I0618192

THE
EFFECTIVE
USE OF
SPIRITUAL
TOOLS

by

S.R. MAYS

S.H.E. PUBLISHING, LLC

The Effective Use of Spiritual Tools

For information contact:

www.shepublishingllc.com | info@shepublishingllc.com

Cover and Title Page Design by Michelle Phillips of CHELLD3 3D VISUALIZATION AND DESIGN

ISBN: 978-1-953163-65-3

First Edition: February 2023

10 9 8 7 6 5 4 3 2 1

FOREWORD

My father.... I pause because I can say so many great things about him. He taught me how to love and be loved. He encouraged everyone to be the best version of themselves, even when he may have felt he was at his worst. I say felt because I didn't discover his struggles until I reached my late teens. Therefore, I never knew there was even a worst. To me, he was just DAD. A man. A wise man. A protector and, still today, a hero. I accredit my father primarily for the teachings of my oldest son being a respectful, God-fearing man. And my father is truly my daughter's favorite person in the whole world. Upon completing rehabilitation in 2011, I remember he stayed an additional two months to mentor others, and he's been on a mission ever since. I'm so proud of him. He's my right hand, and I, his left. And I'm so grateful that he remained faithful, obedient, and humbled. But most of all, I'm grateful that God has a purpose for him… and he's walking in it.

From A Daughter's Heart, **Trinette K Mays**

To say that I'm proud is an understatement. The idea of a book was long before its creation. Seeing the actual process of it and watching it come to fruition is amazing. Hardships and life lessons are the catalysts for the development of this project. Like many others, I have watched my dad battle and struggle with addiction. I have also seen him fight and overcome those same struggles. This book should serve not only as a testimony to the realness of God but also to what faith looks like.

From A Son's Heart, **Raynard Lucas**

CONTENTS

PREFACE

This book is the story of how I struggled with years of substance abuse. I think it's important that anyone reading this will see how a person like me, who was so broken down with a hopeless sense of worth, can, with the proper tools, rebuild their life.

My struggles were my own, and everyone is different. But at a young age, I found myself discontented with the joy of living, probably something a lot of young people have felt. I struggled with this feeling because I wanted a more thrilling lifestyle. Sports provided this thrill until I reached high school. Once there I was introduced to pot and alcohol. Not long after came other mind-altering substances.

Today, after many years of abuse and many years trying to overcome substance abuse, I live a drug-free life. There were many struggles and a multitude of wasted opportunities to escape that lifestyle, which at the time left me depressed. Losing the respect of others, especially people close to me, made me feel ashamed.

But what those feelings gave me was a gradual desire to make a change in my life. And I began to look for any small step I could take to help me do so.

Now when I look back, I realize that each step was like finding a tool. One tool would help me start a building foundation, which required more tools in order to become stronger. Eventually I started calling them "spiritual tools" because the more I used them, the stronger my "spiritual foundation" became. Having a solid spiritual foundation is the first step to overcoming any obstacle in life. So, I decided the only way I could have a spiritual foundation was to have our Creator show me how to build it. Asking for His guidance was my first step. Through His guidance not only were other tools provided, but I was given instructions on how to use most of them. Some I did have to figure out myself through trial and error. But eventually I learned how to use the tool of meditation as a guide to understanding the use and purpose of other tools.

I want to encourage anyone reading this to develop and use their own tools. The tools I share in this book can be used effectively. And it is important to note that they can be improved, added to, or upgraded by anyone for accommodation purposes.

THE OPIOID EFFECT

The opioid epidemic raging across America today will impact this country for decades unless those affected directly and indirectly receive necessary guidance tools, such as effective treatment and proactive aftercare.

Through my many years of opioid abuse, I've learned what I hope will provide some insight into the progression of the disease, the mental and physical effects, and a way to overcome and live with the aftereffects caused by years of abuse. I really hope the information is helpful in some way. Hope can be considered a tool.

HOW
IT BEGAN
FOR ME

Although I used heroin for over thirty years, it was not my primary drug of choice for the first two or three years. During that time I used a variety of substances regularly, including alcohol.

In the early years, it was all about feeling good, the rush, the euphoria. And at the time, being a very young man, I sought that feeling every day. In the book *Drugs and Society*, by Glen R. Hanson, Peter J. Venturelli, and Annette

Fleckenstein, the social and psychological basis to the attraction to a particular drug are laid out. Starting out, there was that social and psychological attraction, but it later became more of a physical necessity. There were no limits to my level of use except when it came to needles. (I still have a fear of them.)

At the time the pleasures outweighed the dangers, - of which I was fully aware but still chose to disregard. I maintained that all my senses, physical skills, and brain functions were enhanced by these substances. It was as if I had discovered a way to perform and live life at a very "high" level, completely ignoring the dangers.

THE PHYSICAL DEPENDENCY

As we all know, nothing lasts forever. And as I discovered, there are consequences to everything we do with our lives and to our bodies, good and bad, and I was about to experience the latter.

Since I was using different types of substances, I never knew the physical illnesses I experienced from time to time were being caused by opioid withdrawals. Because I used other substances, the withdrawals were minor and could be eased with other things, such as marijuana, PCP, alcohol, and LSD. It wasn't until heroin became the drug I depended on that I realized what was causing me to feel sick to my stomach, and none of the other drugs I was using made it better.

Over the next twenty-five or so years, I became dependent on the chemicals found in opioids, and without them, I couldn't do even the simplest of functions. I couldn't sleep or eat, and this caused further physical complications. Without restoration and nourishment, there was no energy to fuel the body, mind, and spirit. Certain bodily functions were affected at first, and then at some point, and to different degrees, all functions became affected.

Opioids dull the senses in the body, including the one that recognizes pain. It is possible for someone to develop an underlying physical affliction and not be aware of it, allowing the condition to become worse because it's not being properly treated. Skin rashes often occur, as well as intestinal problems, lung problems, cases of pneumonia, liver disease, kidney infections, immune system breakdowns, and even heart conditions, which sometimes go unnoticed for long periods of time and can lead to lifelong complications and even death. Even if a person is taking prescribed medications for other problems, such as diabetes or hypertension, those conditions can progress without the substance abuser's knowledge. Opioids can reduce the effectiveness of most prescribed medications. Once the withdrawals begin and pain sensors are no longer dulled, there's only one way in the abuser's mind to make the pain of these conditions go away: by self-medicating with anything containing opioids.

As all of this continued to unfold, I gained a lot of firsthand information related to cause and effect, as far as bodily functions go. This knowledge became a tool that I could refer to and later use as a deterrent.

THE MENTAL AND EMOTIONAL EFFECT

Here is an excerpt, titled "The War Begins," from a journal I wrote in October 2002 that may shed some light on how opioids affected me mentally and emotionally.

There are very many battles and many types of battles that must be won to claim victory in this war. My strategy may seem to those who never had to fight this type of war as one of running away from the problem. But when you've been fighting any war and losing every battle, I felt the best thing I should do is to retreat, reassess, reorganize, and regroup before I reengage my enemy, which was my addiction. There is a time to fight and a time to protect.

I believe I need a solid plan and strong determination to successfully do battle against this enemy, especially since I have battled this enemy for over twenty years and have lost considerably more battles than I have won. I begin to wonder if I can ever win this war before time runs out. Yet I know this is a war that must be won because to lose will mean certain death.

During the years of my many, many battles, my body has taken a physical and mental beating. They've left me drained. I didn't have the drive or determination needed to withstand the agonizing pains of withdrawals, which occur often, forcing me to retreat. I need some "Divine Intervention," and for this to happen, I'll need to develop some measure of faith.

Fear became a great motivator for me. There was a time when I thought I would never be able to live a drug-free life. But as I wrote in another journal in 2002, "Faith is the single most important quality needed to guide one through any adverse situation."

At the time I was unaware that I needed to use faith as a tool. That's probably why it took almost a decade before I was actually able to begin the process.

What I first needed to do was have a desire to stop the effect opioids had on my life. That desire was what led me to pray to God for help, and if I believed He would help, I needed to not only have faith but also exercise it to strengthen it for it to work. He did put me on the right path.

Recovery for me began in February 2011. Thanks to outside help from a treatment center (which was a challenge in and of itself) and faith in what our Creator could do, plus the desire and determination gained through the prayers of me and my family, I am now and without a doubt will remain substance-abuse-free.

Here is one of the first instances where I realized that prayer is a tool.

RESTORATION

Overcoming opioid abuse can be a lengthy process. It requires patience and dedication. The body takes a beating during the abusive period, but the remarkable thing about the body is its ability to repair itself.

Numerous organs are affected and will need time to readjust to functioning without the opioids. During this period the body should be properly nourished and given time to repair itself. Unfortunately, as a consequence of prolonged substance abuse, some organs cannot be restored to their normal functions without the aid of medical treatments.

Mentally this process can be more challenging. The brain has now been deprived of a chemical that it has become very dependent upon. Also the repeated ritual of devising a means to acquire more drugs and the process one goes through to acquire it and then enjoy it leaves a huge imprint on the mind. This process is habit-forming as well and sometimes lingers long after the abuse has ended. There are still times when this ritual haunts me.

Restoration does not occur overnight, and in the beginning, there may be setbacks. Therefore, persistence is necessary. Be patient, determined, and faithful, and in addition, be prayerful. Praying for guidance will provide a blueprint. These were powerful tools that helped me build a solid foundation for my restoration project. (I will share some of these tools in upcoming articles.)

Now came the task of staying substance free. I knew I would need a pathway with someone or something to guide me, to light the "Way." The pathway for me to have a fulfilled life without opioids was clear. Surviving my experiences was a blessing from God, something I prayed for, and now hopefully, I can help others realize that a "Savior" was sent. Before it was called Christianity, the teachings of Jesus were known as the "Way." He came to provide and show us the "Way" to overcome all the darkness produced and influenced by the demons of this world.

Ephesians 6:12 (NIV) states, "For our struggle is not against flesh and blood, but against the authorities, against the powers of this dark world, and against the spiritual forces of evil in heavenly realms." Addiction is a product of demonic influence.

SOURCES AND RESOURCES

The first time I tried heroin was in 1976. I was twenty years old and, by that time, had already been experimenting with marijuana and psychedelic drugs.

By 1984 heroin had become my drug of choice, and it became the source I'd use to fulfill all my desires. Without the drug I had no desire to accomplish anything, even simple things like hygiene. So now the drug dealer had become a "resource" for the "source" I needed to carry out daily functions.

Other functions that were dependent on the drug included eating, grooming, getting proper exercise, and when the moment occurred sex. Without this resource there was no desire to work a job either, and if I managed to get and hold a job, most if not all the money (resources) went to supply my habit (source). The majority of users cannot and will not work unless that need is sufficiently met.

By the year 2008, I began to realize that unless I did something different to change my way of life, I wouldn't have much of a life to live. I knew the source of my unhappiness, and as with all things in life, change had to begin at the source. So, I decided to seek out a new source.

FINDING A DIFFERENT SOURCE

That new source became *the* source, the source of all there is. I'm referring to the Creator, whom I call my "Source."

Now my Source provides all the *resources* I need for the necessities in life. For example, there were times when I wouldn't eat unless I had been medicated, and food is a necessity. When provisions for the necessities are met, provisions for your desires will also be met. In other words, your resources will primarily come from that Source. This realization came to me once I turned to this Source, and my desires shifted.

So I began to work on strengthening my connection to my Source. I started by asking for little things like peace of mind and a change in my desires. Then came bigger things like a job, my own apartment, and my own car. The more I relied on my Source, the more the quality of my resources improved. This is how recognizing and honoring my Source has affected my life as it is today, eleven years substance free.

Daily meditation often gives me a revelation, and one I'd like to share here is: whomever or whatever you decide to recognize as your source will be the provider of your resources. Material things such as money should not be your source. Money is to be used as a resource. Your employer is only a resource that your source may have sent you to. Everyone knows someone who prayed for a certain job or promotion and got what they prayed for. This is the Source of everything guiding you to the resource you prayed for.

For me there is only one absolute truth: there is only one absolute Source. Our Creator is the source of all there is. Without Him there would be no houses, cars, food, and—more importantly—people. And if none of those existed, there would be no need for currency.

I know many do not believe in a Supreme Being, so my suggestion to those people is to find a source that can bring pure joy and peace and doesn't require artificial stimulation, not only for yourself but for those in the world around you, such as family and friends. But don't be afraid to give faith a try.

I thank my Creator every day that I survived and made it out of the darkness. Now it is my desire to help others find a better source that will improve and maybe save their lives.

I have been in that dark hole of addiction, and I am very grateful that I found the "Way" to get out and stay out.

A WAY OUT

We know that the universe was formed out of darkness. The stars that now light up the sky prove that darkness can be overcome, though not eliminated.

Just as our Creator used light to illuminate the universe and bring it to life, He has placed many among us to be a light amid the darkness that's overtaking others. It is a light emanating from someone anointed to draw lost, wandering souls and those consumed by darkness "to shine upon those who sit in darkness and in the shadow of death" (Luke 1:79). I believe our Creator has given many of us who have overcome the influences of dark forces the task of being a light.

Shining a light in the dark can function as a tool.

A DIFFICULT TASK

Just because someone is anointed to shine a light on a path and lead the lost down this path doesn't mean their journey will be an easy one. In fact, it can be difficult and filled with problems. Christ and the Apostles experienced this, as well as many subsequent anointed individuals. Being a light in today's world means bringing all forms of attention on you. That means criticism along with praise.

WHAT IS THE WAY?

As stated in the book of Genesis, Moses asked the God on the mountain who He was, and part of the Lord's answer was, "I am." That to me means everything that exists is of Him and from Him. Everything starts with and ends with Him. Simply put, He is *all*. This includes the heavens we see and the one we can't see.

The Heaven we can't see is the Kingdom of Heaven, which is God's domain. It is His desire that the kingdom exist here on earth, and it is the responsibility of Christians to bring this about. He also provides a means for our salvation, which will be experienced through the gift of eternal life in the Kingdom of Heaven with Him. And the

"Way" to accomplish this is through the lessons learned by the life and death of His son Jesus Christ. Remember, He lived to demonstrate how we could live a kingdom life here on earth, and then He died for all our sins.

So practicing the teachings of Jesus is the Way to the great "I am" and eternal life. Simply put, Jesus is the Way. He is the light. If we were to send God an email, we would sign it "in the name of Jesus." Through Him we can transmit our prayers and requests for forgiveness to the Almighty. Living life through Jesus is the only way to kingdom living here on earth and to live eternally in the Kingdom of Heaven. Kingdom living will prevent addicts from existing. There is salvation from all abuses.

Study the messages of Christ and apply them as tools.

USING MY SPIRITUAL TOOLS

I think the Bible is supposed to teach us to view things as God does, to act as Jesus did. It's like a tool or key that unlocks the gateway to greater wisdom and understanding, which continues to be revealed to us through revelation, as it was intended to be from the beginning.

The Bible is the basis of understanding. It provides a foundation for overcoming obstacles today, just as it did when it was written. Foundations found in the Bible should be built upon to house the issues of yesterday, today, and tomorrow. The Bible is not antiquated, as some have alleged.

Allowing for any discord or disorder to exist within you alters your principles. Once this happens Satan uses this alteration to hijack or hack your personality.

Improper conduct is a disorder and a gateway, and Satan uses it to infect a person through mental or physical illness; a system's primary function, such as a government's ability to govern fairly; or basic principles, such as love and kindness. This infection, if left unchecked, will surely spread throughout the system. Expressed claims of discord or disorder are like passwords that allow Satan access. Protect your health, personality, and principles, or your system, with the Word of God antivirus tools so that when Satan attempts to gain access, he will get an "access denied" code.

SPIRITUAL AWARENESS

Our state of awareness today should always raise our level of consciousness tomorrow. So a heightened state of awareness will produce a heightened state of consciousness. It's how we evolve spiritually, physically, and socially, and it's supposed to occur naturally.

Imagine observing every instance from two thousand years ago and two thousand years from now simultaneously. Our Creator is capable of this awesome feat. So it would stand to reason that He knows what advancements in communication technology are coming and has plans to use them the same way He used the prophets in the Old Testament and some ancient texts.

Our Creator has the ability to use current communication technology. And even though there are dark forces in control of today's technology, spiritual connections are still being made among those of us who choose to become spiritually aware. We get to choose.

There are messages for society that cannot be decoded or understood until we develop a much more sophisticated means to do so, which leads me to believe that ultimately, we will return to the state where our Creator communicates with us directly, as it was meant to be.

SPIRITUAL SIGHT

Dictionary.com defines *foresight* as "the ability to predict or the action of predicting what will happen or what will be needed in the future; seeing things or events before they materialize," kind of like charting the trajectory of a rocket from its launch position and knowing exactly where it will land. It is a tool that I hope to fully develop because I believe it will allow me to gain an edge in many situations concerning my own life.

There is a procedure that should be practiced to accurately use foresight. The process involves looking back to define what has occurred while gaining a better understanding of why. Knowing why something occurred makes it easier to recognize when it reoccurs, thus producing familiarity and the understanding of why it occurred with clarity. This is what is known as *hindsight*. There is a saying, "Hindsight is twenty-twenty," which means looking back and understanding situations or events after they have happened or developed. For example, "Had I known my back would be sore from lifting boxes, I wouldn't have done so." Looking back you now know the possible results or consequences of lifting boxes. Hindsight teaches the same way experience does. Experience of past mistakes should prevent us from repeating them.

This next process is using one's *insight*, which requires accurate intuition. It takes common sense to see what is obvious, but insight provides a deeper and more intuitive understanding of a person or thing. If experience has taught you what happens when you do something good or bad, then whenever that something does occur again, it should become a recognizable pattern from the onset. With this recognition comes a deeper understanding or perspective of a current event. Simply put, it is inside information built on hindsight. This should prepare you for the use of this next tool.

For you to be able to look ahead and predict the outcome of situations, you need to take action in particular situations, outcomes of events, and even another person's abilities and capabilities as well as your own, which should allow you to be better prepared in life. This is the benefit of *foresight*, which is the ability to project an outcome based on information and experiences generated from the first two viewing perspectives.

Those of us who study the teachings of Jesus Christ use discernment to assist with developing all three views or tools. One can never go wrong when relying on His teachings. The Bible is also a great place to study history, and it offers clues on how to view and prepare for eternity, which is the future we as Christians should be living and preparing for.

Let me sum it up this way: **hindsight** is studying the past and clearly seeing what and why something occurred. **Insight** is understanding and immediately recognizing a current event because it has been seen before with obvious results and the ability to clearly understand why something is presently occurring. And **foresight** is using the previous views to accurately foresee an outcome.

How are these tools beneficial? Lessons learned from past experiences should help shape our present lives as a society and as individuals. It's how we progress, and progression is a driving force behind the evolutionary process. My goal is to use these tools to make my life as efficient and productive as possible, and being able to conduct my life using these viewing perspectives allows me to evolve.

Just as with anything, the more you exercise these viewing perspectives the better you will become at using them as tools to avoid many issues, such as mental and physical illnesses, confrontations, personal and professional disputes, and other roadblocks that can slow or prevent progress.

For those of us who study the teachings of Jesus Christ, we should be able to see how He used hindsight, insight, and foresight to deliver His messages because He is "God with us." He is from a place where there is no past, present, or future. He sees every event that has ever happened. He sees what leads to the event, He knows the outcome, and He sees these acts all at once, thus providing Him with hindsight.

So when Jesus spoke and taught, He did so from experience since He was there, providing Him with inside information or insight.

His teachings were intended to shine light on the benefits of accepting His wisdom and the way to apply it in our daily lives. He also provided us with the hope of a future in the Kingdom of Heaven. This is promised to everyone who practices Kingdom Worship and Living. He saw the results of the promise through His foresight.

Anytime there is a recognizable pattern to anything leading up to something that is currently happening, there is a predictable ending. It's probably why older, wiser people can see what a younger person is going through based on their actions, because they've seen it many times before. They recognize it instantly and are likely able to advise that individual on what actions they might take to either bring

prosperity or prevent a catastrophe.

WHERE I AM NOW

Any type of building project requires multiple components from start to finish, including labor. It takes hard work and sacrifice to construct anything from buildings to relationships. It's the same with Kingdom Building, and I have come up with a strategy to use for those who choose to do so.

Here are my strategic tools for salvation.

Need a good place to start? How about building a relationship with the Creator first? Later we will see why I think it should be the first step. Next we need a blueprint, and this is His manual, the Holy Bible. We have the location, here on earth, so now we need to find materials. Since we'll be using only the best for this project, we can also find them in the "Holy Bible Depot" (HBD). Scriptures not only make excellent reading but also provide great kingdom-building material.

Next we'll need tools—again only the best—which also can be found at the HBD. I suggest checking the Gospels of Matthew, Mark, and Luke section. Not only will all the necessary tools be found there but the instructions on how to use them are there also. By the way, all the building components needed for any building project that come from the HBD are already paid for. And there are salespersons available to assist, such as pastors, apostles, ministers, bishops, popes, cardinals, Sunday school teachers, and Bible class teachers, labor included.

A relationship with our Creator should be established first. Faith must be the foundation. Faith in God allows His creativity to flow through every phase of any production. After all, He is *the* Master Creator.

Something I like to think about is what will life be like when the task of building here on earth has been completed and is done as He desires? Maybe all citizens will live in mansions. Literally and figuratively.

THE USE OF SPIRITUAL ALGORITHMS AS A TOOL

Dictionary.com describes an algorithm as a set of instructions for solving a problem or accomplishing a task. So a *Spiritual Algorithm* would be a set of spiritual instructions for solving spiritual problems or accomplishing a spiritual task.

Most if not all the problems humanity experiences originate from the spiritual realm. Poverty, for example, is a spirit used by Satan to steal, kill, and destroy. Fear is another spirit used by Satan. Everything that occurs in the natural world is born out of the spiritual world. Believers are made aware of this through the teachings of Jesus Christ.

Satan recognizes those who are not believers and will design instructions lined with lies and deception and present them as truth to confuse reality. Those who do not believe in the teachings attributed to the Messiah will easily be misled and deceived.

THIS IS HOW SATAN'S ALGORITHM WORKS

Those who do not believe will only see lies and deception as reality, just as with social media platforms, where one Google search for a particular product will show up across all your social media accounts in advertisements for that product and similar ones.

Click on or like antigovernment propaganda and more will show up on your social media newsfeeds. This is how algorithms work, and Satan also uses them to influence one's thinking and beliefs. His instructions disguised as truth are all those who don't know truth will see and accept.

It is also unfortunate that our world leaders, and in some cases religious leaders, are also subjected to the algorithm of misinformation. The good news is that the One who created everything also created the very first "Algorithm."

The "Algorithm of the Holy Spirit" tells believers how to perceive the revelations we are given. Revelation comes from having an overwhelming Spiritual Connection. Satan prefers we rely on information rather than revelation because information can be misleading at times, and without revelation, the truth can be easily hidden.

Technology is a wonderful tool and has greatly improved our way of living to this point. But it can also be used as a weapon of unforeseen consequences.

Spiritual algorithms are generated by the choices we make. Meditate on what Jesus taught and watch the type of revelations that will show up in your algorithms.

Spiritual algorithm is a tool.

THE SPIRITUAL PROXIMITY ALERTS

I am always looking for a better way to explain the benefits of having a relationship with our Creator, and through comparisons I try to demonstrate the significance of this relationship.

In this chapter I'll illustrate this by exploring the use of some of the devices technology has developed to help improve the quality of our lives and compare them to the devices our Creator has developed to also improve our quality of life.

Everyone knows how a garage door opener works. You have to be within a certain proximity to operate it remotely.

There are security systems that sound an alert or light up when their proximity has been breached.

Everyone is aware of Wi-Fi networks and how they work. Some require a passcode to gain access, and some do not, but all require the user to be in proximity of the source. This is the comparison I want to explore for now.

Wi-Fi allows its users to access various communication avenues that lead to a vast amount of information from across the globe. It's a convenient tool we can use without a subscribed plan that some communication providers require at a cost. It is a good comparison because it allows access at relatively no cost.

Our Creator is the source of all there is. We are allowed access to this source on a daily basis. Gaining access does require the belief that our Creator is the sovereign ruler of our lives. Acknowledgment of this is all it costs to access His "system." We also need to show that we are willing to submit to His will. Once we gain access, it will be our faith in Him that will allow us to hear and understand what our assignments are. Faith is like the password needed to access the "supernatural" source that contains unlimited wisdom and power.

All natural occurrences originate first in the supernatural. Ephesians 6:12 (KJV) states, "For we wrestle not against flesh and blood, but against principalities, against powers, against the rulers of the darkness of this world, against spiritual wickedness in high places." We need access to the supernatural to overcome the problems we face in the natural. It does not cost much to believe in His sovereignty. It only requires a little faith to gain access to all the Creator has for us in the supernatural as well as the natural.

In my life I have come to realize that once I accessed my Source, meditation helps me to stay in close proximity to it. Through meditation I can see life with clarity. I have a better understanding of my natural surroundings. And it brings a certain level of calmness. These are just some of the spiritual benefits I experience when I'm in close proximity to my Source. This kind of closeness cannot be gained nor is it possible to be maintained physically unless I'm in close proximity to my Source.

I try to stay in spiritual proximity to my Source, because whenever I'm not, there's a greater possibility of attacks from those unseen forces that are designed to halt my progression or "hack" the program the Creator has developed for me. This has happened to me on many occasions, causing delays, detours, and setbacks in my life.

My desire is to extend the parameters of where I can experience the supernatural benefits of the Holy Spirit. I'm constantly striving to hear His voice clearly outside my current parameters. But it seems like the only thing I can do is continue expanding the parameters, which is the same as growing in faith. Strong faith extends and strengthens the coverage area.

Some proximity alerts use warning sounds, and some systems use lights when the surrounding area has been breached. The better systems use both. "Spiritual" proximity alerts can be tiny voices (sounds), illuminating thoughts (lights), or in some instances both. Our Creator uses these types of alerts to warn us against those seen and unseen forces that are designed to disrupt our lives. Another way these alerts can warn us is in the form of insights gained from hindsight, meaning lessons learned from past experiences.

The proximity alerts system is free to use and can be accessed by all who trust, believe, and obey the Almighty. Faith and submission are the "source codes" needed to activate this system.

The Spiritual Proximity Alerts Warning System is a useful tool.

SPIRITUAL INITIATIVE

Initiative is the power or opportunity to take charge before others do per dictionary.com. It inspires, motivates, and encourages us to make breakthroughs and achieve desired success. It takes initiative to accomplish anything in life, and it must originate from a source. If this source is of a spiritual nature, then it should be considered a "spiritual initiative."

There are many sources in the universe. All initiatives originate from the subconscious or spiritual realm.

How do we recognize this spiritual initiative?

To do so you must be connected to a spiritual source, and my source is the Creator of everything. Being connected allows you to hear and understand the instructions from your source. Like a source code.

WHAT IS A SOURCE CODE?

For computers, it is a fundamental component of a computer program that is created by a programmer and can be read and easily understood by a human being.

Let's say our Creator created a program for us to download the information onto our human hard drives. Understanding this code allows us to receive revelations directly from our source and is easily understood. This requires prayer and meditation, which could be considered passcodes to access this program.

LIVING UNDER PROVIDENCE

What is providence and how can it impact our lives?

Providence is the protective care of our Creator that can guide us to the destination or planned purpose He has for us.

SHARED REVELATION

Our Creator has a purpose for all who believe in His sovereignty. We may not *see* how it will happen, and for the most part, we will only *see* what is right in front of us. When all you *see* is what you *see*, then you do not *see* all there is to be *seen*. For us to *see* what that purpose is, we are to walk by *faith* and not by *sight*.

To add to this thought, this quote was shared with me by my sister Elder Rhonda Taylor: "Our focuses shift according to the level of our struggles and we begin to rely more on what we can see and fix on our own. Lack of trust, lack of endurance, lack of wisdom and knowledge (Not good)."

Elder Rhonda also said, "Faith grows! The more we study and learn of Him, our faith increases…"

Developing faith is key to understanding what it is our Creator has planned for us. Once it is developed, it has to be acted on. This is what walking by faith means. Jesus came to demonstrate how to develop and practice faith. Here are two candid metaphors of how we should do so.

When I read in Revelation 1:8, 21:6, and 22:13 where God says to John, "I am Alpha and Omega, the beginning and the end, the first and the last," I realized that in between those periods of time, He had provided for us a means to go through the ups and downs we all would experience in our lives. That means is called the Holy Spirit, which Jesus came to deliver. So whenever those inevitable times of difficulty occurred, we were to call on the Holy Spirit to carry us or deliver us through. Here's another reminder from Elder Rhonda: "Choose ye this day whom you will serve. His word teaches us to trust Him in all things at all times." Metaphorically speaking, calling on the Holy Spirit to get us to where we need to be is like calling an Uber or Lyft. And the only thing it will cost is faith.

Another practice for those who desire to live under providence can be found in the book of Proverbs 3:5–6: "Trust in the Lord with all thine heart; and lean not unto thine own understanding. In all thy ways acknowledge Him, and He shall direct thy paths." To this verse, my son Ray writes, "We often believe we have the ability to control every outcome, which in most case leads to worry, and when we realize we have limited control is when we must trust that God is in full control."

This second metaphorical analogy is designed to give another example of what living under providence provides.

There is a difference between an athlete who participates in the high-jump competition and one who participates in the pole-vault competition. Their goals are to attempt to elevate their bodies as high as they possibly can over a bar that is set at a particular height.

Now let's compare these competitions to the ones we experience daily in our lives where we try to elevate ourselves to the best heights possible. For most of us, it can be difficult.

The high jumper utilizes his own abilities gained through training to jump as high as he can. But the pole vaulter can jump at least twice as high as the high jumper because he is assisted by a very long pole, which he uses to vault himself over a much higher bar.

We should all have a bar or goal set for ourselves in life. But even with all our skill and training, we sometimes find it difficult to reach the heights we desire. I like the way Elder Rhonda puts it: "What limits man's ability to receive from God and experience results (like the heights I made reference to) is our free will to choose what we trust Him with and lack of wisdom and knowledge." This is why it is important to trust the Holy Spirit. It can act like the pole vaulter's pole that he uses for that extra thrust needed to achieve the necessary altitude to overcome the obstacle, which in his case is the high bar. But for the one living under providence, it provides the additional wisdom and knowledge to help us achieve heights that we wouldn't have without it. In this example the Holy Spirit is the metaphorical pole.

Recognizing the sovereignty of our Creator and practicing trust in Him and obeying His will is a sure way to experience providence in our lives.

I would like to thank my sister Elder Rhonda Taylor and my son Mr. Raynard Lucas for their contributions.

INSPIRATION THROUGH DIVINE MEDITATION

People have often asked me, "What do you gain from meditation?" The easy answer is that I can connect with my "Source" to get answers to my questions or a revelation on something that will help me better understand the Creator's point of view. In other words, I try to see everything the way the Almighty sees it. Meditation brings me revelation, information, and confirmation, which brings me better understanding.

But what is really remarkable to me is that meditation gives me a better understanding of my dreams and visions, of which I've had a few, some that have left me in a state of awe afterward.

One of the first of these kinds of dreams occurred many years ago. During that time I was a substance abuser who really believed that that would be my way of life until the end of it.

I was at home one night lying in bed trying to fall asleep after indulging in my daily habit for most of the day. I didn't remember falling asleep, but I had this dream that left me shaken when I awoke.

In the dream I was back in the basement of my mother's house, which before a remodel was just a full basement with a laundry and furnace area in the rear that was walled off from the front of the basement with a door to allow for entry. When I lived there as a teenager, I slept just on the other side of the wall that separated the two areas.

In my dream I was asleep, and in the middle of the night, I was awakened by a noise I heard coming from the furnace room. When I got up to investigate, I opened the door to the utility area of the basement and was stunned to see the sun shining in a blue sky. Mind you, I was in the basement of a two-story building, and there was no first or second floor, just sunshine and blue sky.

Right at that moment, I knew what was happening, and I began to shake from fear. There I was, an almost middle-aged man who was currently committing all types of sin, and I was about to be judged by the Almighty. I was terrified. I recall trembling so much that my legs got weak and couldn't support me anymore. Down on my knees I went. The only thing I felt was left for me to do was prepare myself for the next step. Where did I go from there? I knew I was in deep trouble.

So I finally got up the courage—even though I was still terrified—to ask, "What do you want me to do?" All I heard was a soft but very clear voice say, "Just live your life." This was a relief to hear, especially since I was expecting to spend eternity in a "very bad place," starting at that very moment.

At the time I was using a combination of substances and committing adulterous acts daily, so for me to hear this from the Creator of everything was puzzling to me. What did that mean, "just live your life"? It wasn't until years later, after the substance abuse and through meditation, that I was able to understand what this dream meant.

Every individual is given a life and a choice of how to live that life. It became clear later on that the Creator was not present to judge me at that time but to remind me of His presence at all times. He allows us to live a way of life of our own choosing, and for me, there was no need to ponder the consequences He had in store for me at that moment. He knew that I had been made aware of the consequences from the teachings I received as a kid from family members who already knew Christ. I just had to choose, at that moment, the life I wanted to live. Still it would be years before I actually chose a different path.

Now that I have changed the way I live my life, I have discovered the benefits of having a relationship with the Almighty. I have a greater understanding of the world around me, which helps me to peacefully navigate through the pains of society. There may not be a special plan for me, but I get to be the architect of my own success in whatever I choose to do in life as long as I allow my Source to guide me. Meditation on that particular spiritual encounter was the tool that brought me to this revelation.

Meditations have often revealed to me, in some instances, what living in the spiritual realm is like. There was another instance just a few years ago where I lay down and closed my eyes—as I always do—and asked, "What is Heaven like?" Immediately my mind was taken to a place where I found myself standing with a group of individuals who were listening to someone handing out assignments. There was no verbal communication among them, but somehow, I was able to determine that they were being given very important tasks to carry out. I could not "hear" their specific assignments, but I sensed their eagerness to comply.

As I stood there, I wondered if I would be given an assignment, but it never happened. Instead I found myself in what I could only describe as a kitchen, but there was no food being served. This was the most immaculately kept, spot-free kitchen I had ever seen. Everything there was a very illuminating white, and those who were present were also dressed, so to speak, in the same bright light. But what struck me the most was that there were items like trash cans—which one would find in any kitchen—but these so-called trash cans were the most immaculately clean vessels that I had ever seen. That was where my tour ended.

I call it a tour because I asked, "What is Heaven like?" and I believe the Creator granted me a tour. Meditation helped me analyze this spiritual encounter.

I believe the group of individuals I mentioned earlier were receiving their assignments from who I could feel in my spirit was Jesus himself. And there was no assignment for me because I was just a tourist.

The tour of the "kitchen" symbolized how everything prepared in Heaven is done to perfection and is done so by spiritual beings. I will leave it up to readers to determine what and how whatever has been prepared in the heavens by the Holy Spirit will affect their lives. Every individual may have a "meal" specifically prepared for them.

I think the cans—I really can't call them trash cans, but it's all I can relate them to—were there just for me. I think this means there is no waste of any kind in Heaven—

no time and no wasted efforts. Readers of this account will and should be able to do their own assessments of what all this means. Meditation is a tool that may help.

I firmly believe in meditation. Just recently I reached out to my Source for guidance as I moved into another phase of my life. All I saw was a door being opened in front of me.

Another vision from when I was still trying to free myself from substance abuse showed me in a jail cell, but this cell had only three sides. With me in this cell were some of the people who I associated with who were also prisoners of substance abuse. It wasn't a situation where I had to break out or even open a door. All I needed to do was walk out and be delivered. I struggled to get out of that cell for years. I had to find the courage to go through the process of being delivered, and I needed to gain this courage from a Source that has always been present and waiting for me to choose the life that deep down inside of me I always wanted to live.

What I have just shared are the dreams and visions that had a significant impact on my life and how I have used them to help strengthen my connection to my Source who is the Creator of all there is.

What this should demonstrate is that anyone in any situation can use meditation to help understand those situations. I began to practice it many years ago, even as I was under the influence of illegal substances and conducting immoral acts. Meditation showed me that no matter what your situation in life is, our Creator is always there for those who choose to seek Him out. I had to learn that involving Him in my life, even though He had no special purpose for it, has provided me with the revelations, information, and a clearer understanding through confirmations of what I can accomplish when I seek His guidance. I have chosen to use prayer and meditation as my primary means to connect to my Source. I ask for guidance through prayer and seek answers through meditation.

Unlocking My Destiny

Recently I had a vision where I was approaching a wooden door. As I approached this door, I realized that it had transformed from wood to steel, though not just a plain steel door: it was a steel vault door similar to one used in banks.

At first I was a bit puzzled by this, but as I looked back over my life, especially the last few years, it became clear what was happening.

Everyone knows the symbolism of what doors represent. In my case, I had been asking for some direction from our Creator concerning my next step in life, which I felt I was ready to take.

For some, doors are opened for them. But for others, doors don't open unless we open them ourselves. I think I would identify with the latter group.

I believe this because in my past there were times when opportunities were presented to me and I did not act immediately or at all, causing me to miss opportunities. So doors were not going to open up for me. They were still there, but because of my passiveness in the past, I would have to open those doors myself.

We learn from the teachings of the Bible that when our Creator delivers a message, at times He will send confirmation that it was He who was the author of the message. Confirmation is the key to being confident that the message comes directly from the Source. And for true believers trained in hearing His words, this confirmation erases any doubt. I am still learning this process.

So now I understand why this symbolic door is there. It's because I have gone to my Source and asked Him for the purpose He has for me and the directions on how to achieve this purpose. Thus the door, or another opportunity depending how you look at it.

Now given my past with doors, not knowing His plans for me, and knowing He knows what my desires are, I believe that I'm going to have to prove to Him that I have the courage and determination to trust and obey whatever it is I am instructed to do, meaning I'm going to have to put in more effort this time in order to see what lies ahead on the other side of this door. That's probably the reason the door has transformed from wood to steel, making it harder for me to open this time. Opening this door would be the same as breaking into a safe in a bank with only my hands and no combination. It probably would have been a lot easier to open if it was still just a wooden door. It appears that I'm the reason this is going to be harder than it has to be.

This is why faith is needed. It is the combination, key, or password that will unlock any barrier.

In some cases a door can be viewed as a gateway, leading to a path. And depending on a person's particular need, the path can contain perils. Satan has doorways and pathways. I have gone through his doors and traveled some of his paths—drugs, alcohol, sex, and more—and I suffered mightily. For me these were alleyways going nowhere, leading to barriers.

The lesson for me is to be grateful that He still allows me to open doors, despite my past negligence, which, I admit, was due to me being unsure if it was my Source who provided the opportunities or if they were a manifestation of my own selfish desires. And if I had created them, I believed I could recreate them myself at any time. Now I understand surrender. By submitting to His will, doors will appear.

Opening this steel door and whatever it represents will be a test of determination, willpower, and above all else, *faith*. I cannot give up. The door must be opened in order for me to receive my instructions. And because I haven't given up, I have been directed to write this book.

How a Can Seed Be Planted in Concrete?

For those of us who study the teachings of the Bible, we understand the benefits of sowing seeds. In the Gospel of

Luke 6:38 of the Easy-to-Read Version (ERV) Bible, Jesus teaches the value of seed sowing: "Give to other people and God will give to you. He will give to you even more than you gave. He will fill your pockets until no more will go in."

In this discussion I'm going to share my thoughts on five particular points pertaining to the relevance of seed sowing that I hope some of you will consider discussing:

1. There are good and bad seeds. What does concrete represent in the context of this discussion?

2. Why should we plant seeds in one another and what can they produce?

3. Why would someone want to plant seeds in concrete, considering how difficult it is to do so compared to planting in soil?

4. Can it be done and how do you go about doing so?

5. What special tools are needed to plant seeds in concrete?

What Are Some Good Seeds and What Are Some Bad Seeds?

We all know how plants grow and the process involved in making them grow, starting with the planting of a seed. The soil in which it's planted is important as well. Planting seeds in properly cultivated soil yields healthy, high-quality plants.

Seeds, when planted, grow all types of things. This also occurs with seeds planted in the spirit. Everyone is aware of the impact "seeds of doubt" can have when planted in someone's mind and heart. The type and quality of seeds planted in spiritual soil will determine the type and quality of the thinking and actions that come out of the spirit. A seed can be an idea that inspires one's thinking and/or motivates the heart. Every achievement of humankind began with an idea in the mind or a feeling of the heart. Also many of the horrible actions recorded throughout history are the results of seeds planted in the mind and the hearts of mankind.

Seeds planted by Satan and those who are controlled by him are considered to be seeds of discord.

In the Gospel of Mark 4:28 (KJV), he is quoting Jesus when he states, "For the earth bringeth forth fruit of herself, first the blade, then the ear, after that the full corn in the ear." What this is saying is that without outside influence, which could contaminate the soil and affect the harvest, the earth will naturally bring forth fruit. The same applies to humankind. Satan wants to contaminate our soil because he knows that every seed planted in it will grow contaminated products.

Seeds planted by mankind into one another can be good seeds or bad seeds. This is why it's important that we are mindful of the kind of seeds we sow and where we sow them. I think pastors, preachers, teachers, or anyone in leadership should cultivate the human soil, meaning the spirit, before seeds can be planted. This prepares us to have a seed planted in our spirit at any moment of our lives.

Evangelism should be used as a tool to cultivate. Cultivating the spirit can be done by teaching lessons from the Bible.

Concrete in this discussion is a metaphor and represents a person who has a layer of resistance to what the lessons of the Bible are meant to teach. There are individuals who, for various reasons, have multiple layers of resistance that may be as difficult to penetrate as concrete.

Why Should We Plant Seeds in One Another, and What Can They Produce?

We have all heard of what is known as the golden rule: "Do unto others as you would have others do unto you." We should keep this in mind when we sow seeds into a person's life. Words are seeds that can impact our lives in various ways. Using improper words can result in a bad harvest, or worse. In other words, we don't want to give a bad report and wind up dying in the wilderness because of it. Like the spies who came back and gave a bad report, a bad confession given with our mouths can produce bad incidents in our lives (Numbers 14:37). Seeds of obedience produce blessings. Seeds of disobedience produce punishments. Good seeds planted in good soil nurtured by faith will grow good fruit. Be careful what you say to and about one another as well as about yourselves. Plant good seeds.

Why would someone want to plant seeds in concrete?

Many are struggling with a variety of obstacles in life. There are those who struggle with various forms of abusing others and being abused. Deception is a tool used by those who are abusers, and there are many forms of abuse that take place in our society. Not only are there abuses by our political leaders, but now we are beginning to witness abuse in our churches by some of their leaders. So I can see why some individuals have hardened their minds and hearts (or soil) to the worded messages (or seeds) we hear from some of our political and spiritual leaders. It is the deception by those who have been elected and chosen to represent and guide us that has caused mistrust in both church and state institutions. Mistrust causes a hardening to develop around one's heart, mind, and spirit. As hard as concrete.

This type of hardening will also prevent new seeds of hope and enlightenment from being planted in someone's life. It makes it harder for the seeds of mistrust that have already sprouted to be rooted out and replaced. A heart covered by concrete is a very dark place. Light does not penetrate concrete in the same manner that enlightenment may not reach a hardened spirit. Those whose hearts have been hardened and are struggling with life are the ones who need the knowledge of salvation or seeds of hope the most.

Can It Be Done, and How Would It Be Done?

These are the easiest questions to answer.

Reaching someone with a hardened heart can be very difficult. Some have been hardened for so long that there are multiple layers of concrete to break through.

It may not be fair, but it may be easier to cultivate someone who has never known Christ and His teachings than it is to recultivate someone who once was a believer. These individuals tend to be the ones with the most layers of resistance or concrete. So I believe that the only way a seed can be planted in anyone who has a hardened heart is for the Creator Himself to plant it. How would He do it? By allowing them to have a "God encounter." A direct encounter with our Creator leaves no doubt that He is exactly who He says He is. No one who has ever had this type of encounter came out of this experience the same person as they were before it. No one. It takes an act of God to remove the concrete surrounding a hardened heart.

What Special Tool Is Needed to Plant Seeds in Concrete?

A direct encounter with the Creator can break through any barrier. His approach to those layers of resistance is like using a metaphorical jackhammer on the metaphorical concrete. I know this from personal experience. Only He wields the tool that can break through any and all barriers.

We were given the commandment by God to help or "honor" one another. And we can do so through the sowing of spiritual and in some cases material seeds. Unfortunately, because Satan rules this world, there are those whose spirits cause them to sow seeds of discord.

Helping one another means that as believers we may at times have to use our armor, helmets, and chest plates and bring the anointed oil as our tools in order to help in the cultivation process, a process that should always take place before our Creator has to step in and resolve the issue. As His servants we are to do all that we humanly can to help those who do not know the "Way" out of the darkness produced by the abuses and deceptions that Satan has unleashed onto humanity, which has caused many hearts and minds to be hardened, some as hard as concrete. We as believers are to demonstrate how to use this armor as a tool against darkness, just as Jesus did. Once this is done, the rest is left up to our Creator, who, as I said, is the metaphorical jackhammer when it comes to breaking through metaphorical concrete.

IN CLOSING

The Bible teaches the proper planting of seeds and what the fruits of the harvest can provide. No one who has faith in this process should struggle with things such as health, relationships, and wealth. Words are seeds; good deeds are seeds. This is why we have to let our words and deeds be an example. We are to plant seeds everywhere we go so when they grow, they will produce more seeds. As the process evolves, the fruits should become better and stronger. Planting seeds to grow more plants is like using spiritual tools to build better and stronger individuals. Spiritual planting is setting the supernatural foundation for a fulfilling, natural life.

About the
AUTHOR

S.R. Mays was born in Chicago, Illinois, in 1956. His mother had him at a very young age, so he practically lived with his godparents while his mom finished school.

Mays had a simple upbringing throughout grammar school. By the time he reached high school, he had nine siblings. It was in his first year of high school when his father passed away, and at that moment, life for him would be altered. Mays was the oldest, so I was counted on to help with his younger sisters and brothers. During his second year of high school, he started drinking alcohol before and after school. Mays was trying to change his perception of the situation. He had begun to feel that he wasn't having enough fun as a teenager. By his senior year in high school, he drank and smoked pot. A year after his graduation in 1974, he was introduced to heroin. Soon he began experimenting with other substances.

In 1976 Mays became a father for the first time. He also started his first real job at a printing company that year. In 1979 he married for the first and only time, and in 1982 his second child was born. By 1985 the marriage had ended. And by 1987, when the printing company closed, May's substance abuse intensified. Also, in 1987 he met someone, and in 1988 his third child was born. He continued to struggle with substance abuse until 2011. Since then, Mays has remained substance abuse-free, thanks to hard work and the support of his mother Margaret and his siblings Saundra, and Catherine, the twins Sharon and Shelly, Rhonda and her twin Rondale, Kenneth, and his half-brother Bobby.

Mays greatest motivation came from his two oldest children, Ray and Trinette, who have remained constant with their motivation and support. And most importantly, he gives thanks to the Creator. The Creator gave him his family; without them, he could not have survived the thirty-plus years of substance abuse.

Currently, Mays time is spent motivating others through the lessons he has learned over those thirty-plus years. His days are filled with thinking of ways to help our youth and young adults through some of life's struggles using the tools he writes about in this book. Mays tries to be a better person each day than he was the day before. He always tells people he's grateful to wake up each day, and everything after he wakes up is a bonus.

Introducing a very grateful and humble servant, **S. R. Mays**